To

From

The Power of a Praying® Parent
by Stormie Omartian

Published by Garborg's™, a brand of DaySpring Cards, Inc.
Siloam Springs, Arkansas

Design by Garborg Design Works

ISBN 1-58061-490-6

January 1

Our children's lives don't ever have to be left to chance.
We can start right now—this very minute, in fact—
making a positive difference in our children's future.
It's never too early and never too late. At every stage
of their lives our children need and will greatly
benefit from our prayers.

December 31

The power you have as a praying parent is God's power. Your prayers release that power to do God's will. It's always available, it's never in limited supply and the only restrictions are due to lack of faith that God will answer. And even then, God's grace is such that when we don't feel we have much faith, the faith we do have is like a mustard seed—enough to grow into something big.

January 2

Pour out your heart like water
before the face of the Lord.
Lift your hands toward Him
For the life of your young children.

LAMENTATIONS 2:19

December 30

And let us not grow weary while doing good, for in due season we shall reap if we do not lose heart. Therefore, as we have opportunity, let us do good to all, especially to those who are of the household of faith.

GALATIANS 6:9-10

January 3

The key is not trying to do it all by ourselves all at once, but rather turning to the expert parent of all time—our Father God—for help. Taking one step at a time, we must cover every detail of our child's life in prayer. There is great *power* in doing that, far beyond what most people imagine. In fact, don't ever underestimate the power of a praying parent.

December 29

Pray that the principle of giving–out of love, as to the Lord, in faith, *with wisdom* and Holy Spirit guidance– be instilled in the hearts and minds of your children, because as they live accordingly, they are guaranteed to be richly blessed and fulfilled.

January 4

We need to declare ourselves to be in full partnership with God. *He* can shoulder the heaviness of the burden and provide wisdom, power, protection, and ability far beyond ourselves. Our job is to discipline, teach, nurture, and "train up a child in the way he should go," knowing that "when he is old he will not depart from it" (Proverbs 22:6).

December 28

Lord, may my child have a relationship with You, Lord, that is truly his/her own—not an extension of mine or anyone else's. I want the comfort of knowing that when I'm no longer on this earth, his/her faith will be strong enough to keep him/her "steadfast, immovable, always abounding in the work of the Lord" (1 Corinthians 15:58).

January 5

We are to depend on God to enable us to raise our child properly, and He will see to it that our child's life is blessed. One thing I have learned is that I should not try to force my own will on my child in prayer. I have found it's better to pray more along the lines of "Lord, show me how to pray for this child. Help me to raise him Your way, and may Your will be done in his life."

December 27

Love is the greatest virtue. It's even greater than faith. But faith is where it begins. That's why we need to pray that as faith increases in our children, they will become God's instruments of giving.

January 6

They shall not labor in vain,
Nor bring forth children for trouble;
For they shall be the descendants
of the blessed of the Lord,
And their offspring with them.

Isaiah 65:23

December 26

Therefore I say to you, whatever things you ask when you pray, believe that you receive them, and you will have them.

MARK 11:24

January 7

My husband and I recognize the hand of God on our own children's lives, and they readily acknowledge it as well. For it's the power of God that penetrates a child's life when a parent prays.

December 25

Children who have faith have distinctly different characteristics from those who don't. They are more confident, more motivated, happier, more positive about the future, and more giving of themselves. A person of faith is filled with God's love and looks for opportunities to share that love with others.

January 8

The righteous man walks in his integrity;
His children are blessed after him.

PROVERBS 20:7

December 24

The father of the righteous will greatly rejoice,
And he who begets a wise child will delight in him.
Let your father and your mother be glad,
And let her who bore you rejoice.

PROVERBS 23:24-25

January 9

Prayer is acknowledging and experiencing the presence of God and inviting His presence into our lives and circumstances. It's seeking the *presence* of God and releasing the *power* of God, which gives us the means to overcome any problem.

December 23

Lord, You have said in Your Word that You have "dealt to each one a measure of faith" (Romans 12:3). I pray that You would take the faith You have planted in my child and multiply it. May the truth of Your Word be firmly established in his/her heart so that faith will grow daily and navigate his/her life.

January 10

Whatever you bind on earth
will be bound in heaven,
and whatever you loose on earth
will be loosed in heaven.

MATTHEW 18:18

December 22

Without faith it is impossible to please Him, for he who comes to God must believe that He is, and that He is a rewarder of those who diligently seek Him.

HEBREWS 11:6

January 11

When we pray, we are humbling ourselves before God and saying, "I need Your presence and Your power, Lord. I can't do this without You." When we don't pray, it's like saying we have no need of anything outside of ourselves. Praying in the name of Jesus gives us authority over the enemy and proves we have faith in God to do what His Word promises.

December 21

Kids without faith have a harder time in life. Kids without faith have no positive motivation, no sense of purpose, and no hope for being any different than they are. They don't know that Jesus died for them (Romans 5:8) and that they are God's children (John 1:12), who are loved, and have a special purpose and calling (1 Corinthians 7:22), and a bright future (1 Corinthians 2:9), and because of that they are sure winners (Romans 8:37).

January 12

Most assuredly, I say to you, whatever you ask the Father in My name He will give you.

JOHN 16:23

December 20

Happy is the man who finds wisdom,
And the man who gains understanding;
For her proceeds are better than the profits of silver,
And her gain than fine gold.
She is more precious than rubies,
And all the things you may desire
cannot compare with her....
Her ways are ways of pleasantness,
And all her paths are peace.
She is a tree of life to those who take hold of her,
And happy are all who retain her.

PROVERBS 3:13-15,17-18

January 13

Praying not only affects *us*, it also reaches out and touches those for whom we pray. When we pray for our children, we are asking God to make His presence a part of their lives and work powerfully in their behalf.

December 19

Lord, help my child to see that all the treasures of wisdom and knowledge are hidden in You and that You give of them freely when we ask for them. As he/she seeks wisdom and discernment from You, Lord, pour it liberally upon him/her so that all his/her paths will be peace and life.

January 14

You did not choose Me, but I chose you and appointed you that you should go and bear fruit, and that your fruit should remain, that whatever you ask the Father in My name He may give you.

JOHN 15:16

December 18

When wisdom enters your heart,
And knowledge is pleasant to your soul,
Discretion will preserve you;
Understanding will keep you,
To deliver you from the way of evil.

PROVERBS 2:10-12

January 15

Our prayers are never lost or meaningless. If we are praying, something is happening, whether we can see it or not. All that needs to happen in our lives and the lives of our children cannot happen without the presence and power of God. Prayer invites and ignites both.

December 17

Lord, I know that much of my child's happiness in life depends on gaining wisdom and discernment, which Your Word says brings long life, wealth, recognition, protection, enjoyment, contentment, and happiness. I want all those things for him/her, but I want them to come as blessings from You.

January 16

The effective, fervent prayer of
a righteous man avails much.

JAMES 5:16

December 16

Wisdom is the principal thing;
Therefore get wisdom.
And in all your getting, get understanding.
Exalt her, and she will promote you;
She will bring you honor, when you embrace her.

PROVERBS 4:7-8

January 17

It's not enough to pray only for the concerns of the moment; we need to pray for the future, and we need to pray against the effects of past events. As my children were growing, I made an extensive personalized list for each of them. I kept many of those lists, and as I look back at them now and see all the answers to my prayers, I'm overcome with the faithfulness of God to work in the lives of our children when we pray.

December 15

Have you ever had times in your life when you knew God's wisdom was in control and you made the right decision in spite of yourself? I believe it is the wisdom and discernment of God. We want that same wisdom and discernment flowing in our children's lives, for as they grow older they make more and more important decisions without us.

January 18

I can do all things through
Christ who strengthens me.

Philippians 4:13

December 14

The fear of the Lord is the beginning of wisdom,
and the knowledge of the Holy One is understanding.

PROVERBS 9:10

January 19

God is the only one who truly knows what each child needs and what challenges they will face in the future. When we employ God's Word in prayer, we are laying hold of the promises He gives us and appropriating them into the lives of our children.

December 13

Lord, I pray that You would give the gifts of wisdom, discernment, and revelation to my child. Help him/her to trust You with all his/her heart, not depending on his/her own understanding, but acknowledging You in all his/her ways so that he/she may hear Your clear direction as to which path to take (Proverbs 3:5).

January 20

Whatever you ask in My name, that I will do,
that the Father may be glorified in the Son.
If you ask anything in My name, I will do it.

JOHN 14:13-14

December 12

If any of you lacks wisdom, let him ask of God, who gives to all liberally and without reproach, and it will be given to him.

JAMES 1:5

January 21

The battle for our children's lives is waged on our knees. When we *do* pray, we're in the battle alongside them, appropriating God's power on their behalf. If we also declare the Word of God in our prayers, then we wield a powerful weapon against which no enemy can prevail.

December 11

So much of our children's safety and well-being depends on decisions they alone will make. The possible outcome of those decisions can seem frightening to a parent. We can't ever be sure they'll make the right decision unless they have the gifts of wisdom, revelation, and discernment along with an ear tuned to God's voice. The only way to secure any of those things is to seek God for them.

January 22

God's Word is "living and powerful, and sharper than any two-edged sword" (Hebrews 4:12). When you are praying for your child, include an appropriate Scripture verse in your prayer whenever you can, and you'll see mighty things happen.

December 10

Call to Me, and I will answer you,
and show you great and mighty things,
which you do not know.

JEREMIAH 33:3

January 23

The righteous cry out, and the Lord hears,
And delivers them out of all their troubles.

PSALM 34:17

December 9

Lord, I put my child in Your hands this day. Guide, protect, and convict him/her when sin is trying to take root. Strengthen him/her in battle when Satan attempts to gain a foothold in his/her heart.

January 24

Through His Word, God guides us, speaks to us, and reminds us He is faithful. In that way, He builds faith in *our* hearts and enables us to understand *His* heart. This helps us to pray boldly in faith, knowing exactly what is *His* truth, *His* will, and *our* authority.

December 8

You don't have to be forever suspicious of your children, but you do have to be suspicious of the Enemy lurking around waiting to erect a stronghold in their lives.

January 25

Most assuredly, I say to you, he who believes in Me, the works that I do he will do also; and greater works than these he will do, because I go to My Father.

John 14:12

December 7

Though they join forces,
the wicked will not go unpunished;
But the posterity of the
righteous will be delivered.

PROVERBS 11:21

January 26

If we understand the power and authority given to us through Jesus Christ, if we WATCH Him, WAIT on Him, WORSHIP Him, and WALK in obedience to His WORD, WE WILL WIN this battle for our children.

December 6

Lord, show me how to pray when there is something deep in my spirit that is unsettled, disturbed, or troubled about my child. Show me anything that I am not seeing, and let all that is hidden come to light. If there is any action I need to take, I depend on You to show me. Thank You that You help me parent this child.

January 27

If you abide in Me, and My words abide in you, you will ask what you desire, and it shall be done for you.

JOHN 15:7

December 5

I will give you the keys of the kingdom of heaven, and whatever you bind on earth will be bound in heaven, and whatever you loose on earth will be loosed in heaven.

MATTHEW 16:19

January 28

Lord, I submit myself to You. I realize that parenting a child in the way You would have me to is beyond my human abilities. I know I need You to help me. I want to partner with You and partake of Your gifts of wisdom, discernment, revelation, and guidance.

December 4

It doesn't necessarily have to be a child's sins you are sensing. It could be hurt, fear, hopelessness, confusion, envy, selfishness, or pride. It's impossible to guess, so it's best to ask God to reveal it to you. Sometimes we don't have to be any more specific than praying for God to penetrate the lives of our children by the power of His Spirit and deliver them from evil. The point is, don't ignore the warnings.

January 29

Whenever you pray for your child, do it as if you are interceding for his or her life—because that is *exactly* what you are doing. Remember that while God has a perfect plan for our children's lives, Satan has a plan for them too. If we are armed with Scripture, however, he will have to contend with the Word of God.

December 3

Lord, give me wisdom and revelation regarding my child. I know there are areas of Enemy operation which I cannot see, so I depend on You, Lord, to reveal these to me as I need to know them. Speak to my heart.

January 30

Now salvation, and strength, and the kingdom of our God, and the power of His Christ have come, for the accuser of our brethren, who accused them before our God day and night, has been cast down.

REVELATION 12:10

December 2

For though we walk in the flesh, we do not war according to the flesh. For the weapons of our warfare are not carnal but mighty in God for pulling down strongholds, casting down arguments and every high thing that exalts itself against the knowledge of God, bringing every thought into captivity to the obedience of Christ.

2 Corinthians 10:3-5

January 31

Possibly the hardest part of praying for our children is waiting for our prayers to be answered. Sometimes the answers come quickly, but many times they do not. If your child has made poor choices, don't berate yourself and stop praying. Keep communication lines open with your child, continue interceding for him or her, and declare God's Word.

December 1

Lord, thank You that You have promised in Your Word to deliver us when we cry out to You. I come to You on behalf of my child and ask that You would deliver him/her from any ungodliness that may be threatening to become a stronghold in his/her life.

February 1

Do not provoke your children to wrath, but bring them up in the training and admonition of the Lord.

EPHESIANS 6:4

November 30

Have you ever observed something in your child that bothers you but you can't identify what it is? When that happens, don't ignore your God-given instincts. Ask God to reveal what it is you're sensing. We are aligned with the Creator of the universe, who understands perfectly what is going on, and we need to ask Him for wisdom and revelation.

February 2

Y*our* part of the fight is to pray. *God* actually fights the battle. Remember, too, that your fight is not with your child, it's with the Devil. *He* is your enemy, not your child. Stand strong in prayer until you see a breakthrough in your child's life.

November 29

Repent therefore and be converted, that your sins may be blotted out, so that times of refreshing may come from the presence of the Lord.

Acts 3:19

February 3

Take the helmet of salvation, and the sword of the Spirit, which is the word of God; praying always with all prayer and supplication in the Spirit, being watchful to this end with all perseverance and supplication for all the saints.

EPHESIANS 6:17-18

November 28

I pray that my son/daughter will never be able to contain sin within him/her, but rather let there be a longing to confess fully and say, "See if there is any wicked way in me, and lead me in the way everlasting" (Psalm 139:24).

February 4

When things go wrong in our children's lives, we blame ourselves. But it's not being a perfect parent that makes the difference in a child's life. It's being a *praying* parent that makes the difference. And that's something we *all* can be.

November 27

Let the wicked forsake his way,
And the unrighteous man his thoughts;
Let him return to the Lord,
And He will have mercy on him;
And to our God,
For He will abundantly pardon.

ISAIAH 55:7

February 5

If two of you agree on earth concerning anything that they ask, it will be done for them by My father in heaven.

MATTHEW 18:19

November 26

Because no child is perfect, we need to ask God to reveal, expose, or bring to light any hidden sin that has taken root in our children's hearts so it can be dealt with now rather than later when the consequences are far more serious. The time to catch it is now.

February 6

Lord, teach me how to love the way You love. Where I need to be healed, delivered, changed, matured, or made whole, I invite You to do that in me.

November 25

Lord, help my child to understand that Your laws are for his/her benefit and that the confession and repentance You require must become a way of life. Give him/her the desire to live in truth before You.

February 7

If you're aware of a child who doesn't have a praying parent, you can step into the gap right now and answer that need. You can effect a change in the life of any child you care about.

November 24

Sin has a toxic effect. Unconfessed sin weighs us down; it distorts and darkens our image. Confessed sin and a repentant heart bring light, life, confidence, and freedom.

Cast away from you all the transgressions which you have committed, and get yourselves a new heart and a new spirit.

EZEKIEL 18:31

February 8

Behold, children are a heritage from the Lord,
The fruit of the womb is a reward.

PSALM 127:3

November 23

Beloved, if our heart does not condemn us,
we have confidence toward God. And whatever we
ask we receive from Him, because we keep His
commandments and do those things
that are pleasing in His sight.

1 John 3:21-22

February 9

In Jesus' name I ask that You will increase my faith to believe for all the things You've put on my heart to pray for concerning this child.

November 22

Lord, I pray that You would give my child a heart that is quick to confess his/her mistakes. May he/she be truly repentant of them so that he/she can be forgiven and cleansed.

February 10

Submit yourself to God and ask Him to help you be the parent and intercessor He wants you to be. Pray as the Holy Spirit leads *you*, as you listen to His prompting in *your* heart for *your* child.

November 21

Wash me thoroughly from my iniquity,
And cleanse me from my sin....
Create in me a clean heart, O God,
And renew a steadfast spirit within me.
Do not cast me away from Your presence,
And do not take Your Holy Spirit from me.
Restore to me the joy of Your salvation,
And uphold me by Your generous Spirit.

PSALM 51:2,10-12

February 11

A child is a gift to us from God and He cares even more about our child than we do.

Cast...all your care upon Him, for He cares for you.

1 Peter 5:7

November 20

Confession and repentance are two life principles we must insist upon for our children, because unconfessed sin will put a wall between them and God. If sin is not confessed and repented, the child can't be free of the bondage, and that will show on his/her face and his/her personality.

February 12

Lord, may the beauty of Your Spirit be so evident in me that I will be a godly role model. Give me the communication, teaching, and nurturing skills that I must have. Make me the parent You want me to be and teach me how to pray and truly intercede for the life of this child.

November 19

If you forgive men their trespasses,
your heavenly Father will also forgive you.

MATTHEW 6:14

February 13

For you shall go out with joy,
And be led out with peace;
The mountains and the hills
Shall break forth into singing before you.

ISAIAH 55:12

November 18

There is nothing like the tears of joy and release we feel when we come to that place of complete forgiveness before the Lord. It's life-giving because it renews our entire being.

February 14

After the initial pain of releasing our children there comes joy and peace, both for them *and* us. Because we know that, no matter what stage of life our children are in, when we release them to God they are in *good hands*. We know that they will go forth in peace and joy and God will make a way for them.

November 17

Lord, may my child always walk in the light of love and forgiveness. Teach him/her to release the past to You so that he/she can move into all that You have for him/her. In Jesus' name, I pray that he/she will live in the fullness of Your forgiveness for him/her and walk in the freedom of forgiveness in his/her own heart.

February 15

Lord, my child is the biggest "care" I have, and I release him/her into Your hands. Only You can raise him/her right and truly keep him/her safe. I will no longer strive to do it all by myself but will enter into full partnership with You.

November 16

Blessed be the Lord,
For He has shown me His marvelous kindness!

PSALM 31:21

February 16

For this child I prayed, and the Lord has granted me my petition which I asked of Him. Therefore I also have lent him to the Lord; as long as he lives he shall be lent to the Lord.

1 Samuel 1:27-28

November 15

Forgiveness is trusting that God is the God of justice He says He is and saying, “Father, I won’t hold that person to myself with unforgiveness any more.” It’s acknowledging that God knows the truth and allowing Him to be the judge, because He is the only one who knows the whole story.

February 17

The only way to be sure that God *is* in control is to surrender our hold and allow Him full access to their lives. The way to do that is to live according to His Word and His ways and pray to Him about everything. We can trust God to take care of our children even better than we can.

November 14

We cannot get on with our lives and all that God has for us as long as we are bound and tethered to the past. Neither can our children.

One thing I do, forgetting those things which are behind and reaching forward to those things which are ahead, I press toward the goal for the prize of the upward call of God in Christ Jesus.

PHILIPPIANS 3:13-14

February 18

Lord, I come to You in Jesus' name and give my child to you. I'm convinced that You alone know what is best for him/her. You alone know what he/she needs. I release him/her to You to care for and protect, and I commit myself to pray for everything concerning him/her that I can think of or that You put upon my heart.

November 13

One of the best things we can do to help our children stay free of unforgiveness, besides teaching *them* to be forgiving and praying that they walk in forgiveness, is to get free of unforgiveness ourselves. When I finally learned that forgiveness doesn't make the *other person right*, it makes *you free*, I found great breakthrough in that area.

February 19

If you then, being evil, know how to give good gifts to your children, how much more will your Father who is in heaven give good things to those who ask Him!

MATTHEW 7:11

November 12

Lord, according to Your Word I pray that my child will love his/her enemies, bless those who curse him/her, do good to those who hate him/her so that he/she may enjoy all Your blessings (Matthew 5:44-55).

February 20

When we release our children into the Father's hands and acknowledge that He is in control of their lives and ours, both we and our children will have greater peace.

November 11

As a part of honoring father and mother and receiving the promise of long life and blessing that accompanies that commandment, every child needs to forgive both parents for their imperfections and anything they may have done that was hurtful.

February 21

The mercy of the Lord is from
everlasting to everlasting
On those who fear Him,
And His righteousness to children's children,
To such as keep His covenant,
And to those who remember
His commandments to do them.

PSALM 103:17-18

November 10

Let all bitterness, wrath, anger, clamor, and evil speaking be put away from you, with all malice. And be kind to one another, tenderhearted, forgiving one another, just as God in Christ forgave you.

EPHESIANS 4:31-32

February 22

Thank You, Lord, for the precious gift of this child. Because Your Word says that every good gift comes from You, I know that You have given him/her to me to care for and raise. Help me to do that.

November 9

Lord, I pray that You would enable my child to live in ongoing forgiveness. Teach him/her the depth of Your forgiveness toward him/her so that he/she can be freely forgiving toward others.

February 23

And whatever we ask we receive from Him, because we keep His commandments and do those things that are pleasing in His sight.

1 John 3:22

November 8

Whenever I have to apologize to my children for something, I tell them I need to hear them say, "I forgive you." I don't do that just because *I* need to *hear* it; I do it because *they* need to *say* it and be completely released.

February 24

We can't be everywhere. But God can. We can't see everything. But God can. We can't know everything. But God can. No matter what age our children are, releasing them into God's hands is a sign of our faith and trust in Him and is the first step toward making a difference in their lives. Prayer for our children begins there.

November 7

Lord, may my child have one mate for life who is also his/her closest friend. May they be mutually loyal, compassionate, considerate, sensitive, respectful, affectionate, forgiving, supportive, caring, and loving toward one another all the days of their lives.

February 25

When you pass through the waters,
I will be with you;
And through the rivers,
they shall not overflow you.
When you walk through the fire,
you shall not be burned,
Nor shall the flame scorch you.

ISAIAH 43:2

November 6

He who finds a wife finds a good thing,
And obtains favor from the Lord.

PROVERBS 18:22

February 26

Lord, thank You that I can partner with You in raising my child and that I don't have to do it alone. I'm grateful that I can have clear directions from Your Word and wisdom as I pray to You for answers.

November 5

Lord, help my child to realize that unless You are at the center of a marriage, it will never stand. Unless You bless it, it won't be blessed. For Your Word says, "Unless the Lord builds the house, they labor in vain who build it" (Psalm 127:1). I pray that You would build the marriage around which their house is established.

February 27

Often our most urgent and fervent prayers regarding our children are for their protection. It's hard to think about other aspects of their lives if we are worried sick over their personal safety.

November 4

This is the day the Lord has made;
We will rejoice and be glad in it.

PSALM 118:24

February 28

For He shall give His angels charge over you,
To keep you in all your ways.
In their hands they shall bear you up,
Lest you dash your foot against a stone.

PSALM 91:11-12

November 3

I pray that my child will trust You with all his/her heart and lean not on his/her own understanding; that he/she will acknowledge You in all his/her ways so that You will direct his/her path (Proverbs 3:5-6).

February 29

Being a praying parent doesn't mean that nothing bad will ever happen to your children or that they will never experience pain. They *will*, because pain is a part of life in this fallen world. But the Bible assures us that our prayers play a vital part in keeping trouble from them.

November 2

I believe that marriages can literally be made in heaven when we pray to the ultimate matchmaker. It's not bridal consultants and caterers who set the bride and groom on the right path. Consulting God and following His leading does that. And only prayer keeps our children continually seeking God's will instead of following their own emotions.

March 1

He delivers me from my enemies.
You also lift me up above those who rise against me;
You have delivered me from the violent man.

PSALM 18:48

November 1

I pray that my son/daughter will be submissive enough to hear Your voice when it comes time to make a marriage decision, and that he/she will make that decision based on what You are saying and not just fleshly desire.

March 2

Lord, I lift my child up to You and ask that You would put a hedge of protection around him/her. Protect his/her spirit, body, mind, and emotions from any kind of evil or harm.

October 31

But from the beginning of the creation, God "made them male and female." "For this reason a man shall leave his father and mother and be joined to his wife, and the two shall become one flesh"; so then they are no longer two, but one flesh. Therefore what God has joined together, let not man separate.

MARK 10:6-9

March 3

"No weapon formed against you shall prosper,
And every tongue which rises against you in judgment
You shall condemn.
This is the heritage of the servants of the Lord,
And their righteousness is from Me,"
Says the Lord.

Isaiah 54:17

October 30

Lord, I pray that unless Your plan is for him/her to remain single, You will send the perfect marriage partner for my child. Send the right husband/wife at the perfect time, and give him/her a clear leading from You as to who it is.

March 4

Disasters can occur anywhere. The point is to pray and trust God to answer. Things happen when we pray that will not happen when we don't. What might happen, or might *not* happen, to our children if we don't pray today? Let's not wait to find out. Let's get on our knees now.

October 29

Next to their decision to receive Jesus, marriage is the most important decision our children will ever make. And because only God knows who will make the best marriage partner for anyone, He should be consulted first and He should give the final answer.

March 5

God is our refuge and strength,
A very present help in trouble.
Therefore we will not fear,
Even though the earth be removed,
And though the mountains be
carried into the midst of the sea;
Though its waters roar and be troubled,
Though the mountains shake with its swelling.

PSALM 46:1-3

October 28

Lord, may Your grace enable my child to be committed to staying pure so that he/she will receive Your crown of life.

Blessed is the man who endures temptation; for when he has been approved, he will receive the crown of life which the Lord has promised to those who love Him.

JAMES 1:12

March 6

Thank You, Lord, for Your many promises of protection. Help my child to walk in Your ways and in obedience to Your will so that he/she never comes out from under the umbrella of that protection. Keep him/her safe in all he/she does and wherever he/she goes. In Jesus' name, I pray.

October 27

But to you who fear My name
The Sun of Righteousness shall arise
With healing in His wings.

MALACHI 4:2

March 7

Because you have made the Lord, who is my refuge,
Even the Most High, your dwelling place,
No evil shall befall you,
Nor shall any plague come near your dwelling;

PSALM 91:9-10

October 26

We must pray for our children to trust God and not their unreliable emotions, so that they will walk with wisdom and avoid this dangerous trap. We must pray for them to live God's way. One of God's ways for our lives is sexual purity, and the foundation for it is laid at a very young age.

March 8

I'm convinced it's never too soon to start praying for a child to feel loved and accepted–first by God, then by family, then by peers and others.

October 25

No temptation has overtaken you except such as is common to man; but God is faithful, who will not allow you to be tempted beyond what you are able, but with the temptation will also make the way of escape, that you may be able to bear it.

1 Corinthians 10:13

March 9

For I am persuaded that neither death nor life, nor angels nor principalities nor powers, nor things present nor things to come, nor height nor depth, nor any other created thing, shall be able to separate us from the love of God which is in Christ Jesus our Lord.

ROMANS 8:38-39

October 24

Lord, may my child long for *Your* approval, Lord, and not allow sexual sin in his/her life at any time. Deliver him/her from any spirit of lust bringing temptation to fail in this area. Put a Holy Spirit alarm in him/her that goes off like a loud, flashing siren whenever he/she steps over the line of what is right in Your sight.

March 10

Rejection brings out the worst in people. Love and acceptance bring out the best. Knowing that God loves and accepts us changes our lives.

October 23

We can't wait until our children are teenagers to pray about sexual purity, just as we can't wait until then to instruct them that life works better when we live God's way. Today is the day to pray.

March 11

But God demonstrates His own love toward us, in that while we were still sinners, Christ died for us.

ROMANS 5:8

October 22

The body is not for sexual immorality
but for the Lord, and the Lord for the body.

1 Corinthians 6:13

March 12

Lord, I pray for my child to feel loved and accepted. Penetrate his/her heart with Your love right now and help him/her to fully understand how far-reaching and complete it is.

October 21

Lord, I pray that You will keep my child sexually pure all of his/her life. Give him/her a heart that wants to do what's right in this area, and let purity take root in his/her personality and guide his/her actions.

March 13

For God so loved the world that He gave His only begotten Son, that whoever believes in Him should not perish but have everlasting life.

John 3:16

October 20

Next to catastrophic injury, death, and eternal hell, sexual immorality is the most dreaded possibility for our children's lives. I know that with sexual sin the fullness of God's presence, peace, blessing, and joy is sacrificed. The price is way too high.

March 14

Even though it is God's love that is ultimately most important in anyone's life, a parent's love (or lack thereof) is perceived and felt first. Parental love is the first love a child experiences and the first love he/she understands.

October 19

Therefore if the Son makes you free, you shall be free indeed.

JOHN 8:36

March 15

In this the love of God was manifested toward us, that God has sent His only begotten Son into the world, that we might live through Him. In this is love, not that we loved God, but that He loved us and sent His Son to be the propitiation for our sins. Beloved, if God so loved us, we also ought to love one another.

1 JOHN 4:9-11

October 18

Lord, give my child discernment and strength to be able to say “no” to things that bring death and “yes” to the things of God that bring life. Enable him/her to choose life in whatever he/she does, and may his/her only addiction be to the things of God.

March 16

Lord, help my child to abide in Your love. Manifest Your love to this child in a real way today and help him/her to receive it.

As the Father loved Me, I also have loved you; abide in My love.

JOHN 15:9

October 17

Your children are *yours* and *not* the Devil's, and you can make a case for them before the throne of God. *You* have the power *and* the authority. Satan doesn't. Rebuke his lies by the power invested in you through Jesus Christ your Savior, who is Lord over everything in your life, including your child.

March 17

Parental love is often the means by which children actually open themselves to God's love and come to understand it early in life. That's why from the time our children are born, we should pray, "God, help me to really love my child the way You want me to and teach me how to show it in a way he/she can understand."

October 16

I have set before you life and death,
blessing and cursing; therefore choose life,
that both you and your descendants may live.

DEUTERONOMY 30:19

March 18

We have known and believed the love that God has for us. God is love, and he who abides in love abides in God, and God in him.

1 John 4:16

October 15

Lord, speak to my child's heart, show him/her the path he/she should walk, and help him/her see that protecting his/her body from things that destroy it is a part of his/her service to You.

March 19

I have loved you with an everlasting love.

JEREMIAH 31:3

October 14

The draw of the flesh and the Devil's plans are a lot stronger than we'd like to think. In a moment of weakness, such as is possible for all of us, we can end up doing something we never thought we would. Only the power of God, through prayer, can make the difference.

March 20

I pray that You would help me to love this child unconditionally the way You do, and enable me to show it in a manner he/she can perceive.

October 13

For if you live according to the flesh you will die; but if by the Spirit you put to death the deeds of the body, you will live.

Romans 8:13

March 21

Cause me to hear Your
loving kindness in the morning,
For in You do I trust.

Psalm 143:8

October 12

Lord, I pray that You would keep my child free from any addiction—especially to alcohol or drugs. Make him/her strong in You, draw him/her close, and enable him/her to put You in control of his/her life.

March 22

Along with prayer, children need to see love manifested toward them with eye contact, physical touch (a pat, a hug, a kiss), and with loving acts, deeds, and words.

October 11

Satan wants our children, and he'll take them any way he can. Alcohol, drugs, and other addictions are some of his most successful lures. In fact, the attack against our children is so great that they cannot stand against it without our support. The good news is that *with* our support, prayer covering, and teaching, they can stand firm.

March 23

The love of God has been poured out in our hearts
by the Holy Spirit who was given to us.

ROMANS 5:5

October 10

Therefore, if anyone is in Christ,
he is a new creation;
old things have passed away;
behold, all things have become new.

2 Corinthians 5:17

March 24

Lord, with each day that my child grows in the confidence of being loved and accepted, release in him/her the capacity to easily *communicate* love to others.

October 9

I pray that my son/daughter will not inherit any bondage from his/her earthly family, but will "inherit the kingdom prepared for [him/her] from the foundation of the world" (Matthew 25:34). Thank You, Jesus, that in You the old has passed away and all things are new.

March 25

For you are a holy people to the Lord your God; the Lord your God has chosen you to be a people for Himself, a special treasure above all the peoples on the face of the earth.

DEUTERONOMY 7:6

October 8

In Jesus' name we can be set free from any family bondage, and by the power of the Holy Spirit we can refuse to allow it any place in our children's lives.

March 26

One of God's main purposes for your life is to fill you with so much of His love that it overflows onto others. Praying for your child will not only be a sign of that love in your heart, it could also be the very means by which that love is multiplied to overflowing.

October 7

The Spirit of the Lord God is upon Me,
Because the Lord has anointed Me
To preach good tidings to the poor;
He has sent Me to heal the brokenhearted,
To proclaim liberty to the captives,
And the opening of the prison
to those who are bound.

ISAIAH 61:1

March 27

Blessed be the God and Father of our Lord Jesus Christ, who has blessed us with every spiritual blessing in the heavenly places in Christ, just as He chose us in Him before the foundation of the world, that we should be holy and without blame before Him in love.

EPHESIANS 1:3-4

October 6

Thank You, Jesus, that You came to set us free from the past. We refuse to live bound by it. Thank You, Father, that You have "qualified us to be partakers of the inheritance of the saints in the light" (Colossians 1:12).

March 28

As my child comes, Lord, to fully understand the depth of Your love for him/her and receives it into his/her soul, make him/her a vessel through which Your love flows to others. In Jesus' name I pray.

October 5

A good way to see family bondage *broken* in your child is to see it broken in you first. The best place to start is to identify any sin in your life. The next thing to do is identify any bondage in your parents or grandparents that you feel could be affecting you or your children and pray about that also.

March 29

We are bound to give thanks to God always for you, brethren beloved by the Lord, because God from the beginning chose you for salvation through sanctification by the Spirit and belief in the truth.

2 Thessalonians 2:13

October 4

Blessed be the God and Father of our Lord Jesus Christ, who according to His abundant mercy has begotten us again to a living hope through the resurrection of Jesus Christ from the dead, to an inheritance incorruptible and undefiled and that does not fade away, reserved in heaven for you, who are kept by the power of God through faith for salvation ready to be revealed in the last time.

1 PETER 1:3-5

March 30

Above all else, we want our children to come to a knowledge of who God really is and to know Jesus as their Savior. When that happens, we know their eternal future is secure; we know that when they die, we will see them again in heaven. What a wonderful hope that is!

October 3

If there is any work of the Enemy in my family's past that seeks to encroach upon the life of my child, I break it now by the power and authority given me in Jesus Christ.

March 31

Behold, I stand at the door and knock. If anyone hears My voice and opens the door, I will come in to him and dine with him, and he with Me.

REVELATION 3:20

October 2

When we see things we don't like about ourselves reflected in our children, we can do something about it. And if we've observed these same traits in our parents and grandparents, we can be *especially* diligent to pray specifically about breaking this generational bondage.

April 1

Lord, I bring my child before You and ask that You would help him/her grow into a deep understanding of who You are. Open his/her heart and bring him/her to a full knowledge of the truth about You.

October 1

For you did not receive the spirit of bondage again to fear, but you received the Spirit of adoption by whom we cry out, "Abba, Father." The Spirit Himself bears witness with our spirit that we are children of God, and if children, then heirs—heirs of God and joint heirs with Christ.

ROMANS 8:15-17

April 2

Above all else, know God's the One who'll never leave you.
Look to Him above all else.
He is love you can depend upon, a heart set to care.
If in the darkest night you should be lost, He will be there.
He's the Everlasting Father, In His hands you'll never fall.
He's the One who holds it all,
Above all else.

ABOVE ALL ELSE, LYRICS BY STORMIE OMARTIAN

September 30

Lord, You have said in Your Word that a good man leaves an inheritance to his children's children (Proverbs 13:22). I pray that the inheritance I leave to my children will be the rewards of a godly life and a clean heart before You.

April 3

This is the will of Him who sent Me, that everyone who sees the Son and believes in Him may have everlasting life; and I will raise him up at the last day.

John 6:40

September 29

Unlike physical traits, spiritual tendencies are something we don't have to inherit. That's because they are usually nothing more than the unquestioned acceptance of a firmly entrenched lie of the Enemy. We can choose to break away from them through prayer and the power of the Holy Spirit.

April 4

Lord, You have said in Your Word, "If you confess with your mouth the Lord Jesus and believe in your heart that God has raised Him from the dead, you will be saved" (Romans 10:9). I pray for that kind of faith for my child.

September 28

Now may the God of hope fill you with all joy and peace in believing, that you may abound in hope by the power of the Holy Spirit.

Romans 15:13

April 5

No matter what age your children are, it's never too early or too late to start praying for their salvation. We want our children to open the door of their hearts to Jesus and experience God's kingdom, both in this life and forever after.

September 27

Negative emotions should not be a way of life. We should look to the Lord because "He brought forth his people with joy" (Psalm 105:43 KJV). He will bring forth our children in like manner if we ask it of Him.

April 6

For this is good and acceptable in the sight of God our Savior, who desires all men to be saved and to come to the knowledge of the truth.

1 Timothy 2:3-4

September 26

If you keep My commandments, you will abide in My love, just as I have kept My Father's commandments and abide in His love. These things I have spoken to you, that My joy may remain in you, and that your joy may be full.

JOHN 15:10-11

April 7

Once our children have received the Lord, we must continue praying for their relationship with Him. We want our children to always be "filled with the knowledge of His will in all wisdom and spiritual understanding" and to "walk worthy of the Lord, fully pleasing Him, being fruitful in every good work and increasing in the knowledge of God" (Colossians 1:9-10).

September 25

Lord, plant Your Word firmly in my child's heart and increase his/her faith daily. Enable him/her to abide in Your love and derive strength from the joy of the Lord this day and forever.

April 8

We know that the Son of God has come and has given us an understanding, that we may know Him who is true; and we are in Him who is true, in His Son Jesus Christ. This is the true God and eternal life.

1 John 5:20

September 24

You will show me the path of life;
In Your presence is fullness of joy;
At Your right hand are pleasures forevermore.

PSALM 16:11

April 9

I pray that my child will live a fruitful life, ever increasing in the knowledge of You. May he/she always know Your will, have spiritual understanding, and walk in a manner that is pleasing in Your sight. I pray that You would pour out Your Spirit upon my child this day.

September 23

The joy of the Lord is rich and deep and causes anyone who walks in it to be likewise. That's because joy doesn't have anything to do with happy circumstances; it has to do with looking into the face of God and knowing He's all we'll ever need.

April 10

And I will pray to the Father, and He will give you another Helper, that He may abide with you forever— the Spirit of truth, whom the world cannot receive, because it neither sees Him nor knows Him; but you know Him, for He dwells with you and will be in you.

JOHN 14:16-17

September 22

For His anger is but for a moment,
His favor is for life;
Weeping may endure for a night,
But joy comes in the morning.

PSALM 30:5

April 11

Thank You, Lord, that You care about my child's eternal future even more than I do and that it is secure in You. In Jesus' name I pray that he/she will not doubt or stray from the path You have for him/her all the days of his/her life.

September 21

Lord, I pray that my child be given the gift of joy. Let the spirit of joy rise up in his/her heart this day and may he/she know the fullness of joy that is found only in Your presence. Help him/her to understand that true happiness and joy are found only in You.

April 12

And this is the testimony: that God has given us eternal life, and this life is in His Son.

1 John 5:11

September 20

And my soul shall be joyful in the Lord;
It shall rejoice in His salvation.

PSALM 35:9

April 13

The Bible says, "Children, obey your parents in the Lord, for this is right. 'Honor your father and mother,' which is the first commandment with promise: 'that it may be well with you and you may live long on the earth'" (Ephesians 6:1-3). The fact that we can affect the length and quality of our children's lives is reason enough to pray, instruct, and discipline.

September 19

Sadly, many young people today suffer with depression. This doesn't have to happen. Don't allow your child to be stuck with a sad, depressed, angry, moody, or difficult personality. Pray them out of it.

April 14

Lord, I pray that You would give my child a heart that desires to obey You. Put into him/her a longing to spend time with You, in Your Word and in prayer, listening for Your voice.

September 18

For the weapons of our warfare are not carnal but mighty in God for pulling down strongholds, casting down arguments and every high thing that exalts itself against the knowledge of God, bringing every thought into captivity to the obedience of Christ.

2 Corinthians 10:4-5

April 15

Obedience brings great security and the confidence of knowing you're where you're supposed to be, doing what you're supposed to do. The Bible promises that if we are obedient we will be blessed. We want our children to walk in obedience so that they will have confidence, security, long life, and peace.

September 17

I pray that my child will so love the Lord with all his/her heart, soul, and mind that there will be no room in him/her for the lies of the Enemy or the clamoring of the world. May the Word of God take root in his/her heart and fill his/her mind with things that are true, noble, just, pure, lovely, of good report, virtuous, and praiseworthy (Philippians 4:8).

April 16

Lord, Your Word instructs, "Children, obey your parents in all things, for this is well pleasing to the Lord" (Colossians 3:20). I pray that You would turn the heart of this child toward his/her parents and enable him/her to honor and obey father and mother so that his/her life will be long and good.

September 16

Be anxious for nothing, but in everything by prayer and supplication, with thanksgiving, let your requests be made known to God; and the peace of God, which surpasses all understanding, will guard your hearts and minds through Christ Jesus.

PHILIPPIANS 4:6-7

April 17

Remember, your battle is not with your son or daughter. "For we do not wrestle against flesh and blood, but against principalities, against powers, against the rulers of the darkness of this age, against spiritual hosts of wickedness in the heavenly places" (Ephesians 6:12). Your battle is with the Enemy. The good news is that Jesus has given you authority "over all the power of the enemy" (Luke 10:19).
Don't be afraid to take advantage of that.

September 15

A big part of having a sound mind has to do with what goes into it. Filling our minds with what is out in the world brings confusion. Filling our minds with the things of God—especially His Word—brings clarity of thought and peace of mind.

God is not the author of confusion but of peace.

1 Corinthians 14:33

April 18

Lord, make my child uncomfortable with sin. Help him/her to know the beauty and simplicity of walking with a sweet and humble spirit in obedience and submission to You.

September 14

Do not be conformed to this world, but be transformed by the renewing of your mind, that you may prove what is the good and acceptable and perfect will of God.

Romans 12:2

April 19

My son, hear the instruction of your father,
And do not forsake the law of your mother;
For they will be a graceful ornament on your head,
And chains about your neck.

PROVERBS 1:8-9

September 13

One of the many wonderful things about receiving Jesus and being filled with the Holy Spirit is that, along with every other blessing, we gain a stability and sound-mindedness that cannot be acquired any other way. That's because we are given the mind of Christ.

Let this mind be in you which was also in Christ Jesus.

PHILIPPIANS 2:5

April 20

When you cover your family relationships in prayer, whether it be with children, parents, stepparents, brothers, sisters, grandparents, aunts, uncles, cousins, husband, or wife, there will be far fewer instances of strained or severed relationships.

September 12

I will both lie down in peace, and sleep;
For You alone, O Lord, make me dwell in safety.

Psalm 4:8

April 21

Behold, how good and how pleasant it is
For brethren to dwell together in unity!

PSALM 133:1

September 11

Lord, thank You for promising us a sound mind. I lay claim to that promise for my child. I pray that his/her mind would be clear, alert, bright, intelligent, stable, peaceful, and uncluttered.

April 22

Lord, I pray for my child and his/her relationship with all family members. Protect and preserve them from any unresolved or permanent breach. Fill his/her heart with Your love and give him/her an abundance of compassion and forgiveness that will overflow to each member of the family.

September 10

You will keep him in perfect peace,
Whose mind is stayed on You,
Because he trusts in You.

ISAIAH 26:3

April 23

Let us pursue the things which make for peace and the things by which one may edify another.

ROMANS 14:19

September 9

The world and the Devil are making every effort to control your child's mind. The good news is that you have the authority to resist those efforts. If your child is young, you have authority over what he puts *into* his mind. But most important of all, you have the power of prayer. So, even if your child is beyond your daily influence, you can pray for his mind to be sound and protected.

April 24

God tells of all the wonderful things that will happen when we fast and pray. He says, “You shall raise up the foundations of many generations; and you shall be called the Repairer of the Breach” (Isaiah 58:12). God wants us to restore unity, to maintain the family bonds in the Lord, and to leave a spiritual inheritance of solidarity that can last for generations.

September 8

There is no fear in love; but perfect love casts out fear, because fear involves torment. But he who fears has not been made perfect in love.

1 John 4:18

April 25

Be of one mind, having compassion for one another; love as brothers, be tenderhearted, be courteous.

1 Peter 3:8

September 7

Thank You, Lord, for Your promise to deliver us from all our fears. In Jesus' name I pray for freedom from fear on behalf of my child this day.

April 26

Jesus said, "Blessed are the peacemakers, for they shall be called the sons of God" (Matthew 5:9). I say let's be peacemakers. Let's begin by praying for those closest to us—our children—and branch out from there.

September 6

For God has not given us a spirit of fear,
but of power and of love and of a sound mind.

2 Timothy 1:7

April 27

Now may the God of patience and comfort grant you to be like-minded toward one another, according to Christ Jesus, that you may with one mind and one mouth glorify the God and Father of our Lord Jesus Christ.

ROMANS 15:5-6

September 5

Because we have Jesus, we and our children never have to live with or accept a spirit of fear as a way of life.

April 28

Lord, teach my child to resolve misunderstandings according to Your Word. And if any division has already begun, if any relationship is strained or severed, Lord, I pray that You will drive out the wedge of division and bring healing. Give him/her a heart of forgiveness and reconciliation.

September 4

Lord, wherever there is real danger or good reason to fear, give my child wisdom, protect him/her, and draw him/her close to You. Plant Your Word in his/her heart. Let faith take root in his/her mind and soul as he/she grows in Your Word.

April 29

Now I plead with you, brethren, by the name of our Lord Jesus Christ, that you all speak the same thing, and that there be no divisions among you, but that you be perfectly joined together in the same mind and in the same judgment.

1 Corinthians 1:10

September 3

Parents have the authority and power through Jesus Christ to resist that spirit of fear on their child's behalf. *Fear* doesn't have power over us. *We* have power over *it*. Jesus gave us authority over *all* the power of the Enemy (Luke 10:19).

April 30

Parents often have gut-level feelings about their children's friends. When that happens, ask God for Holy Spirit-inspired discernment and pray accordingly.

September 2

The Lord is my light and my salvation;
Whom shall I fear?
The Lord is the strength of my life;
Of whom shall I be afraid?

PSALM 27:1

May 1

Lord, I lift up my child to You and ask that You would bring godly friends and role models into his/her life. Give him/her the wisdom he/she needs to choose friends who are godly, and help him/her to never compromise his/her walk with You in order to gain acceptance.

September 1

Lord, flood my child with Your love and wash away all fear and doubt. Give him/her a sense of Your loving presence that far outweighs any fear that would threaten to overtake him/her. Help him/her to rely on Your power in such a manner that it establishes strong confidence and faith in You.

May 2

God's Word clearly instructs us: "Do not be unequally yoked together with unbelievers. For what fellowship has righteousness with lawlessness?" (2 Corinthians 6:14). That doesn't mean our children can never have a nonbelieving friend. But there is clear implication that their closest friends, ones to whom they have strong ties, should be believers.

August 31

Fear not, for I am with you;
Be not dismayed, for I am your God.
I will strengthen you, Yes, I will help you,
I will uphold you with My righteous right hand.

ISAIAH 41:10

May 3

Lord, enable my child to walk with wise friends and not have to experience the destruction that can happen by walking with foolish people.

August 30

When Jesus was at sea with His disciples and a storm came up, He responded to their terror by saying, "Why are you fearful, O you of little faith" (Matthew 8:26). He wants us, like them, to believe that our boat won't sink if He's in it with us.

May 4

One of the greatest influences in our children's lives will be their friends and role models. How can we not pray about them?

August 29

Oh, how great is Your goodness,
Which You have laid up for those who fear You,
Which You have prepared for those who trust in You
In the presence of the sons of men!

PSALM 31:19

May 5

Blessed is the man
Who walks not in the counsel of the ungodly,
Nor stands in the path of sinners,
Nor sits in the seat of the scornful.

PSALM 1:1

August 28

Lord, Your Word says, "I sought the Lord, and He heard me, and delivered me from all my fears" (Psalm 34:4). I seek You this day, believing that You hear me, and I pray that You will deliver my child from any fear that threatens to overtake him/her.

May 6

I pray that You would teach my child the meaning of true friendship. Teach him/her how to be a good friend and make strong, close, lasting relationships. May each of his/her friendships always glorify You.

August 27

He shall cover you with His feathers,
And under His wings you shall take refuge;
His truth shall be your shield and buckler.
You shall not be afraid.

PSALM 91:4-5

May 7

Be kindly affectionate to one another with brotherly love, in honor giving preference to one another.

Romans 12:10

August 26

Fear is something that comes upon us the moment we don't believe that God is able to keep us, or all we care about, safe. Fear easily strikes children because they can't always discern what's real and what isn't. Our comfort, reassurance, and love can *help* them; but praying, speaking the Word of God in faith, and praising God for His love and power, can *free* them.

May 8

Fearing God means having a deeply committed respect, love, and reverence for God's authority and power. It means being afraid of what life would be like without Him and being grateful that because of His love we'll never have to experience such despair. It means hungering for all that God is and all that He has for us.

August 25

Have mercy upon me, O God,
According to Your lovingkindness;
According to the multitude of Your tender mercies,
Blot out my transgressions.
Wash me thoroughly from my iniquity,
And cleanse me from my sin.

PSALM 51:1-2

May 9

Lord, I pray for my child to have an ever-increasing hunger for more of You. May he/she long for Your presence—long to spend time with You in prayer, praise, and worship. Give him/her a desire for the truth of Your Word and a love for Your laws and Your ways.

August 24

Lord, put Your complete protection over my child's room so that evil cannot enter here by any means. Fill this room with Your love, peace, and joy. I pray that You, Lord, will make this room a holy place, sanctified for Your glory.

May 10

Oh, fear the Lord, you His saints!
There is no want to those who fear Him.

PSALM 34:9

August 23

Praying through a room is not a superstitious little ritual. This is a powerful claiming of your home, your child, and all aspects of his life for God. It's standing up and proclaiming, "As for me and my house, we will serve the Lord" (Joshua 24:15). It's saying, "My home is sanctified and set apart for God's glory."

May 11

There is so much in the world to divert our children's attention away from the things of God, and the Devil will come to each child with his agenda and plan to see if they will buy into it. But when we do our part to teach, instruct, discipline, and train our children in the ways of God, then our children will develop a hunger for the things of God.

August 22

Therefore, having these promises, beloved, let us cleanse ourselves from all filthiness of the flesh and spirit, perfecting holiness in the fear of God.

2 Corinthians 7:1

May 12

Lord, teach my child to live by faith and be led by the Holy Spirit, having an availability to do what You tell him/her to do. May he/she be so aware of the fullness of Your Holy Spirit in him/her that when he/she is depleted in any way he/she will immediately run to You to be renewed and refreshed.

August 21

When you pray through your child's room, remove anything that is not glorifying to God. God's Word on this should be lovingly explained to the child and, if at all possible, he should be encouraged to remove the offensive articles himself. Explain that for his own peace and blessing he must clean the room of anything that is not of the Lord. Then pray over the room thoroughly.

May 13

Blessed are those who hunger
and thirst for righteousness,
For they shall be filled.

MATTHEW 5:6

August 20

Lord, I invite Your Holy Spirit to dwell in this room, which belongs to my child. You are Lord over heaven and earth, and I proclaim that You are Lord over this room as well. Flood it with Your light and life.

May 14

When we do our part to train our children in the ways of God, they will know that the things of God are top priority. They will become God-controlled and not flesh-controlled. They will long for His ways, His Word, and His presence. They will fear God and live a longer and better life.

August 19

Everyone's house needs a spiritual housecleaning from time to time, especially in the rooms where our children sleep and play. The Bible says if we bring anything detestable into our homes, we bring destruction along with it. A holy housecleaning should be done periodically as a matter of principle, but definitely whenever you feel troubled by something in your child.

May 15

Lord, may a deep reverence and love for You and Your ways color everything my child does and every choice he/she makes. May he/she not be wise in his/her own eyes, but rather "fear the Lord and depart from evil" (Proverbs 3:7).

August 18

A highway shall be there, and a road,
And it shall be called the Highway of Holiness.
The unclean shall not pass over it....
But the redeemed shall walk there,
And the ransomed of the Lord shall return,
And come to Zion with singing,
With everlasting joy on their heads.
They shall obtain joy and gladness,
And sorrow and sighing shall flee away.

Isaiah 35:8-10

May 16

The fear of the Lord is a fountain of life,
To turn one away from the snares of death.

PROVERBS 14:27

August 17

Lord, may a desire for holiness that comes from a pure heart be reflected in all that my child does.

Blessed are the pure in heart, for they shall see God.

MATTHEW 5:8

May 17

Finding a church that is actively teaching God's Word, showing God's love, and sharing God's joy with its children and young people will make a big difference in helping your children develop a hunger for the things of God.

August 16

There is nothing more compelling than children who walk in holiness and purity. Let's pray for our children to be among those who do.

Let no one despise your youth, but be an example to the believers in word, in conduct, in love, in spirit, in faith, in purity.

1 Timothy 4:12

May 18

I pray that my child will be reliable, dependable, responsible, compassionate, sensitive, loving, and giving to others. Deliver him/her from any pride, laziness, slothfulness, selfishness, or lust of the flesh.

August 15

Every branch in Me that does not bear fruit He takes away; and every branch that bears fruit He prunes, that it may bear more fruit.

John 15:2

May 19

I have been crucified with Christ; it is no longer I who live, but Christ lives in me; and the life which I now live in the flesh I live by faith in the Son of God, who loved me and gave Himself for me.

GALATIANS 2:20

August 14

To live purely within the boundaries of God's law is to find wholeness in the total person. That wholeness is what holiness is all about. Children who have a desire for holiness and seek God's enabling power to help them achieve it can never be anything but blessed and fulfilled.

May 20

Start right now by praying for your child to fear God, have faith in Him and His Word, and develop the kind of heart that seeks after Him. This could be the determining factor in whether your child will have a constant struggle living in the flesh or be fulfilled and blessed living in the Spirit.

August 13

Lord, give my child understanding that to live in purity brings wholeness and blessing, and that the greatest reward for it is seeing You.

May 21

I pray that my child will have a teachable and submissive spirit that says "yes" to the things of God and "no" to the things of the flesh. Strengthen him/her to stand strong in his/her convictions.

August 12

Let us pray for our children to be attracted to holiness and purity like a magnet, so that when anything entices them that isn't holy or pure, they detect the pull immediately and are made uncomfortable enough to thoroughly reject it. "For God did not call us to uncleanness, but in holiness" (1 Thessalonians 4:7).

May 22

Blessed are those who keep His testimonies,
Who seek Him with the whole heart!

PSALM 119:2

August 11

Lord, hide Your Word in my child's heart so that there is no attraction to sin. Let Christ be formed in him/her and cause him/her to seek the power of Your Holy Spirit to enable him/her to do what is right.

May 23

Lord, as my child learns to read Your Word, write Your law in his/her mind and on his/her heart so that he/she always walks with a confident assurance of the righteousness of Your commands.

August 10

We want our children to be known for their goodness. We want our children to be attractive to others because of their purity. This doesn't just happen. It must be taught. And although we can do much to teach our children, the real teacher is the Holy Spirit.

May 24

Teach me Your way, O Lord;
I will walk in Your truth;
Unite my heart to fear Your name.
I will praise You, O Lord my God, with all my heart,
And I will glorify Your name forevermore.

PSALM 86:11-12

August 9

Who may ascend into the hill of the Lord?
Or who may stand in His holy place?
He who has clean hands and a pure heart,
Who has not lifted up his soul to an idol,
Nor sworn deceitfully.
He shall receive blessing from the Lord,
And righteousness from the God of his salvation.

PSALM 24:3-5

May 25

Lord, as my child learns to pray, may he/she also learn to listen for Your voice. May there always be a Holy Spirit fire in his/her heart and an unwavering desire for the things of God.

August 8

Lord, I pray that You would fill my child with a love for You that surpasses his/her love for anything or anyone else. Help him/her to respect and revere Your laws and understand that they are there for his/her benefit.

May 26

He who dwells in the secret place of the Most High
Shall abide under the shadow of the Almighty.
I will say of the Lord, "He is my refuge and my fortress;
My God, in Him I will trust."

PSALM 91:1-2

August 7

Children who are taught to live in purity and holiness have distinctly radiant faces and a compelling attractiveness. The Bible says, “Even a child is known by his deeds, whether what he does is pure and right” (Proverbs 20:11).

May 27

Not knowing who God made us to be, trying to be who we are not, or even just *desiring* to be someone else, can only lead to a life of misery, frustration, and unfulfillment. We become the person God created us to be when we ask Him for guidance and then do what He tells us to do.

August 6

There is one who speaks
like the piercings of a sword,
But the tongue of the wise promotes health.

PROVERBS 12:18

May 28

Lord, I pray that You would pour out Your Spirit upon my child this day and anoint him/her for all that You've called him/her to be and do. May it be for this child according to Your Word, that he/she never stray from what You have called him/her to be and do, or try to be something he/she is not.

August 5

Lord, enable my child to always speak words of hope, health, encouragement, and life, and to resolve that his/her mouth will not sin.

May 29

You are a chosen generation, a royal priesthood, a holy nation, His own special people, that you may proclaim the praises of Him who called you out of darkness into His marvelous light.

1 Peter 2:9

August 4

The best way to improve speech is to improve the heart, "For out of the abundance of the heart the mouth speaks" (Matthew 12:34). A heart filled with the Holy Spirit and the truth of the Word of God will produce godly speech that brings life to the speaker as well as the listener. This is where our point of prayer should begin.

May 30

One of the Devil's plans for young people is to get them to compare themselves with others, judge themselves as deficient, and then seek to be someone they were not created to be. Our prayers can block this plan of the Enemy and give our children a clear vision of themselves and their future.

August 3

Pleasant words are like a honeycomb,
Sweetness to the soul and health to the bones.

PROVERBS 16:24

May 31

Eye has not seen, nor ear heard,
Nor have entered into the heart of man
The things which God has prepared
for those who love Him.

1 CORINTHIANS 2:9

August 2

We want our children to speak life. This doesn't mean they can't be honest about negative feelings. But those words should be spoken for the purpose of confession, understanding, and submission to God for healing, not as tools of destruction.

June 1

The biggest part of helping my son and daughter understand who God created them to be is encouraging their relationship with the Lord. I know they will never fully understand who *they* are until they understand who *God* is.

August 1

Lord, may my child speak life and not death. May he/she be quick to listen and slow to speak so that his/her speech will always be seasoned with grace. Equip him/her to know how, what, and when to speak to anyone in any situation.

June 2

Lord, may my child find his/her identity in You, view himself/herself as Your instrument, and know that he/she is complete in You. Give him/her a vision for his/her life and a sense of purpose about what You've called him/her to do.

July 31

Speech that is not godly or not of the Lord, such as, "I'm no good" or "I wish I was dead," does not reflect a heart filled with the Holy Spirit. It reflects the work of darkness. And that is exactly what will play itself out on the stage of your child's life if you don't help him monitor what he says.

June 3

Be even more diligent to make your call and election sure, for if you do these things you will never stumble.

2 PETER 1:10

July 30

Let the words of my mouth
and the meditation of my heart
Be acceptable in Your sight,
O Lord, my strength and my Redeemer.

PSALM 19:14

June 4

God promises to pour out His Spirit on our children. They will be filled with His Spirit and have that inner confidence of knowing they are His. You will see a confident and radiant expression on the face of any child who can say with conviction, "I am the Lord's." Do you want that for your child enough to pray for it?

July 29

Lord, I pray that my child will choose to use speech that glorifies You. Fill his/her heart with Your Spirit and Your truth so that what overflows from his/her mouth will be words of life and not death.

June 5

And we know that all things work together for good to those who love God, to those who are the called according to His purpose.

ROMANS 8:28

July 28

We create a world for ourselves by what we speak. Words have power, and we can either speak life or death into a situation. The Bible says that what we say can get us *into* trouble or keep us *away* from it. It can even save our lives. "He who guards his mouth preserves his life, but he who opens wide his lips shall have destruction" (Proverbs 13:3).

June 6

Children will lie at one time or another. The question is not *if* they will, but whether or not lying will become something they believe they can get away with. If we don't teach our children what God says about lying, they won't know why it's wrong. If we don't pray about this issue now, there will be bigger issues to deal with later.

July 27

I thank my God always concerning you for the grace of God which was given to you by Christ Jesus, that you were enriched in everything by Him in all utterance and all knowledge, even as the testimony of Christ was confirmed in you, so that you come short in no gift, eagerly waiting for the revelation of our Lord Jesus Christ.

1 Corinthians 1:4-7

June 7

Lying lips are an abomination to the Lord,
But those who deal truthfully are His delight.

PROVERBS 12:22

July 26

Each child has special gifts and talents. We need to pray for them to be identified, revealed, developed, nurtured, and used for God's glory.

June 8

Lord, I pray that You will fill my child with Your Spirit of truth. Give him/her a heart that loves truth and follows after it, rejecting all lies as a manifestation of the Enemy.

July 25

Most of all, I pray the gifts and talents You placed in my child be released to find their fullest expression in glorifying You.

June 9

I have no greater joy than to hear that my children walk in truth.

3 John 1:4

July 24

Pray that your child will develop and excel in the gifts and talents God has given him/her, and let him/her know he/she has a unique purpose and significance in this world.

June 10

Pray now that any lying spirit will be uprooted—not only in your children, but in *yourself* as well. We need to reject the way of lying and follow the truth. We need to be an example to our children.

July 23

As each one has received a gift,
minister it to one another, as good stewards
of the manifold grace of God.

1 Peter 4:10

June 11

My soul melts from heaviness;
Strengthen me according to Your word.
Remove from me the way of lying,
And grant me Your law graciously.

PSALM 119:28-29

July 22

When God gives you a glimpse of your child's potential for greatness, love and pray him/her into being that. The Bible says, "Do you see a man who excels in his work? He will stand before kings; he will not stand before unknown men" (Proverbs 22:29).

June 12

I pray that my child will not be blinded or deceived, but always be able to clearly understand Your truth.

July 21

I pray that You would reveal to my child what his/her life work is to be and help him/her excel in it. Bless the work of his/her hands, and may he/she be able to earn a good living doing the work he/she loves and does best.

June 13

Let not mercy and truth forsake you;
Bind them around your neck,
Write them on the tablet of your heart,
And so find favor and high esteem
In the sight of God and man.

PROVERBS 3:3-4

July 20

What gifts and talents has God planted in *your* child? Every child has them. They are there, whether you can see them or not. The Bible says, "Each one has his own gift from God, one in this manner and another in that" (1 Corinthians 7:7). Sometimes it takes prayer to uncover them.

June 14

I pray that Your Spirit of truth will guide my child into all truth. May he/she never be a person who gives place to lies, but rather a person of integrity who follows hard after the Spirit of truth.

July 19

To each one of us grace was given according to the measure of Christ's gift.

Ephesians 4:7

June 15

When He, the Spirit of truth, has come,
He will guide you into all truth.

JOHN 16:13

July 18

Lord, I thank You for the gifts and talents You have placed in my child. I pray that You would develop them in him/her and use them for Your glory. Make them apparent to me and to him/her, and show me specifically if there is any special nurturing, training, learning experience, or opportunities I should provide for him/her. May his/her gifts and talents be developed in Your way and in Your time.

June 16

We have prayed our children through every cold, flu, fever, and injury, and the Lord has always answered. We never hesitate to take them to a doctor when they need it, of course, because we know God heals through doctors, too. The point is to pray first and then, when we are healed, we are not to question or doubt.

July 17

Because the Enemy wants to use our children's gifts for *his* glory, or at the very least keep them from being used for God's purposes, we need to cover them in prayer. Praying for the development of our children's God-given gifts and talents is an ongoing process.

June 17

Is anyone among you sick? Let him call for the elders of the church, and let them pray over him, anointing him with oil in the name of the Lord. And the prayer of faith will save the sick, and the Lord will raise him up.

JAMES 5:14-15

July 16

Every good gift and every perfect gift is from above, and comes down from the Father of lights, with whom there is no variation or shadow of turning.

JAMES 1:17

June 18

Lord, because You have instructed us in Your Word that we are to pray for one another so that we may be healed, I pray for healing and wholeness for my child. I pray that sickness and infirmity will have no place or power in his/her life. And if we are to see a doctor, I pray that You, Lord, would show us who that should be. Give that doctor wisdom and full knowledge of the best way to proceed.

July 15

From the time my children were born, I prayed for God to reveal to us the gifts, talents, and abilities He had placed in them and to show us how to best nurture and develop them for His glory. I asked God what to do about it and waited on Him for the answer.

June 19

Bless the Lord, O my soul,
And forget not all His benefits:
Who forgives all your iniquities,
Who heals all your diseases.

PSALM 103:2-3

July 14

Lord, enable my child to experience the joy of learning more about You and Your world.

May the Lord give you understanding of all things.

2 Timothy 2:7

June 20

One of the main things Jesus wants to be to us is the forgiver of our sins and the healer of our bodies. Let's lay hold of the health and healing He has for our children by praying for it even before the need arises.

Confess your trespasses to one another, and pray for one another, that you may be healed.

JAMES 5:16

July 13

My son, if you receive my words,
And treasure my commands within you...
And lift up your voice for understanding,
If you seek her as silver,
And search for her as for hidden treasures;
Then you will understand the fear of the Lord,
And find the knowledge of God.

PROVERBS 2:1,3-5

June 21

But He was wounded for our transgressions,
He was bruised for our iniquities;
The chastisement for our peace was upon Him,
And by His stripes we are healed.

Isaiah 53:5

July 12

I pray my child will respect the wisdom of his/her parents and be willing to be taught by them. May he/she also have the desire to be taught by the teachers You bring into his/her life.

Apply your heart to instruction,
and your ears to words of knowledge.

PROVERBS 23:12

June 22

Thank You, Lord, that You suffered and died for us so that we might be healed. I lay claim to that heritage of healing which You have promised in Your Word and provided for those who believe. I look to You for a life of health, healing, and wholeness for my child.

July 11

A child's ability and desire to learn cannot be taken for granted. Even while our child is still in the womb we can pray, "Lord, let this child be knit perfectly together with a good, strong, healthy mind and body and be taught by You forever."

June 23

Your light shall break forth like the morning,
Your healing shall spring forth speedily,
And your righteousness shall go before you;
The glory of the Lord shall be your rear guard.

ISAIAH 58:8

July 10

Take firm hold of instruction, do not let go;
Keep her, for she is your life.

PROVERBS 4:13

June 24

Nearly everyone struggles somewhat in the area of proper body care. We do our children a disservice if we don't support them in prayer, as well as guide and instruct them in healthy practices, so that they don't end up miserable.

July 9

Lord, give my child a good mind, a teachable spirit, and an ability to learn. Above all, I pray that he/she will be taught by You, for Your Word says that when our children are taught by You they are guaranteed peace.

June 25

Do you not know that your body is the temple of the Holy Spirit who is in you, whom you have from God, and you are not your own? For you were bought at a price; therefore glorify God in your body and in your spirit, which are God's.

1 CORINTHIANS 6:19-20

July 8

A wise man will hear and increase learning,
And a man of understanding will attain wise counsel.

PROVERBS 1:5

June 26

If your children are young, start praying for them to be attracted to healthful food and to desire to exercise and take good care of their bodies. If your children are older, begin right now to intercede on their behalf.

July 7

If we receive His words and treasure His commands in our heart, if we work at trying to understand and ask God to help us do so, if we seek understanding as fervently as we would search out hidden treasure, then we will find the knowledge of God (Proverbs 2:1-12).

June 27

Lord, I lift my child to You and ask that You would place in him/her a desire to eat healthy food. Help him/her to understand what's good for him/her and what isn't, and give him/her a desire for food that is healthful.

July 6

All your children shall be taught by the Lord,
And great shall be the peace of your children.

Isaiah 54:13

June 28

I beseech you therefore, brethren, by the mercies of God, that you present your bodies a living sacrifice, holy, acceptable to God, which is your reasonable service.

ROMANS 12:1

July 5

Lord, I pray that my child will have a deep reverence for You and Your ways. May he/she hide Your Word in his/her heart like a treasure, and seek after understanding like silver or gold.

June 29

Lord, Your Word says, “You shall know the truth, and the truth shall make you free” (John 8:32). Help my child to see the truth about the way he/she is to live, so that he/she can be set free from unhealthy habits.

July 4

In one way or another, of course, we all have deficiencies. Thankfully, God makes up for our deficiencies with His strength. His Word says, "Not that we are sufficient of ourselves to think of anything as being from ourselves, but our sufficiency is from God" (2 Corinthians 3:5). That is so true.

June 30

Your child needs Holy Spirit guidance and strength to do what's right for his or her body. Your prayers can spare them much defeat, frustration, and heartbreak. Don't you wish you'd had someone praying about this for you?

July 3

Help my child to see that what makes a person truly attractive is Your Holy Spirit living in him/her and radiating outward. May he/she come to understand that true attractiveness begins in the heart of one who loves God.

July 1

Lord, whenever my child struggles may she turn to You and say, "Teach me Your way, O Lord" (Psalm 27:11). Give him/her a vision of his/her body as the temple of Your Holy Spirit. I pray that he/she will value the body You've given him/her and desire to take proper care of it.

July 2

Therefore, whether you eat or drink,
or whatever you do, do all to the glory of God.

1 Corinthians 10:31